HELP!

I NEED MY
SUPERHEROES!

There's a
craZY clown
up to no good.
let's stop him, I think
we should...

We need **superheroes**, i wonder where they are. Let's go and look, they can't have gone far!

ZOE ZOOM

She can fly up into the air.
She's out in the park, I wonder where?

WAYNE WHIZZ

He can zip around, faster than a fly.
Can you spot him,
before he zips by?

LUCKY LIZ

She has a dog called Rover.
She's lucky like a four leaf clover!

CLEVER CARL

He knows everything there is to know.
I wonder where he's decided to go?

BARRY BURP

He has a power of which he's super proud... Barry can burp really loud!

DANGER
SLIPPERY ICE!

SUPERBABY

Her skin is smoother than silk.
She can drink lots and lots and
lots of milk!

PETER POWER

He can blast a hole into the ground.
But, I wonder, can he be found?

SALLY THE STRONG

She's not big, but she's also not small...
she can lift a car, no trouble at all!

TIME TRAVEL TIM

He's in the future, he can travel to
the past... but he doesn't stay long,
so find him fast!

COLIN CARROT

He can see in the dark, just like a
great white shark!

She can spin superfast on the spot.
She's

SHONA SPIN-A-LOT

CONNOR CLAWS!

His fingers are pointy and long... he goes
after the baddies who've done wrong!

ZAPPER ZAC

He's not scared, nor is he shy.
He'll zap the baddies, easy as pie!

SUPERMUM & SUPERDAD

They can't fly or walk on water...
they look after their son and daughter!

You found all the **superheroes**, well done!

NOW they've caught the clown...

We did it, **WE WON!**

A bonus search!
MORE BADDIES!

The three above are hiding in the book. Don't believe me? Go take a look!

THE END!

HELP! BOOKS

Find us on Amazon!

Discover all of the titles available in the series; including these below...

HELP! MY MONSTERS ARE ON THE LOOSE!

HELP! MY PETS HAVE GONE MISSING!

HELP! MY ROBOTS ARE LOST IN THE CITY!

HELP! MY DINOSAURS ARE LOST IN THE CITY!

HELP! I'VE LOST MY TEDDIES!

HELP! THE PIRATE HAS LOST HIS SHIPMATES!

Why not try this awesome spot the difference superhero book?

Featuring 14 fabulous double page scenes, bursting with superheroes!

© 2021 Webber Books

Printed in Great Britain
by Amazon